5th Grade Gumshoe Math

Carlos Treviño Calderón

Calderon Publications ®

Calderon Publications
2401 S Clavel Ave
Weslaco, Texas 78596

ISBN: 9780692025352

Preface

The activities in Gumshoe Math allow your students the opportunity to practice several math concepts in one fun game puzzle at a time. Each puzzle gives the student an opportunity to examine the logic of each clue and its applicability to the final outcome which is the hidden number. These puzzles can be worked independently, in pairs, or in small groups. Critical and analytical thinking is promoted as the students contemplate which digit fits the criteria and where it should be placed within the number. Each clue includes mathematical terms which are essential to mathematical proficiency. This continued exposure to the vocabulary promotes student internalization of, and fluency with, academic vocabulary. Gumshoe Math is a sponge activity that you can use as opening or closing lessons or at any time during your instructional day.

Tips for nabbing a hidden number!

Hidden Number

1. I am a number between 10, 000 and 100,000.
2. I am divisible by five.
3. My ten-thousands digit is prime.
4. My hundreds digit is a factor of eight.
5. All of the digits in my ones/units period are even.
6. My thousands digit is odd.
7. My ten-thousands digit is double my thousands digit.
8. My hundreds digit is greater than five.
9. My ten-thousands digit is even.
10. The sum of all my digits is 15.

Step 1: Read clues 1 and 2. What do those clues tell you?

These two clues are very important because if it's between 10, 000 and 100,000, the greatest number it can be is 99,999 and the least is 10,001 so it must be a 5 digit number. If it's divisible by 5, its ones digit must be either 0 or 5.

You can begin to set this number up as shown below by drawing five blank spaces (one for each digit).

___ ___ , ___ ___ ___
                    0
                    5

Step 2: Now consider clue number 3. The **ten-thousands digit** is prime. What are the prime single digit numbers?

2, 3, 5, and 7

What about clue number 4? What numbers can go in **the hundreds place**?

The factors of eight are 1,8,2,and 4.

Clue number 5 is very important. All of the digits in the **ones/units period** are even. Which of our possible numbers for the **ones place** is even?

Look below at how our number is starting to look.

___ ___ , ___ ___   0
   2   1   0   0
   3   2   2   5
   5   4   4
   7   8   6
                   8

Step 3: Clues 6 and 7 are again very important. If the **ten-thousands digit** is a number that has been doubled then that makes it even and divisible by 2. Clue number 9 reemphasizes this.

The only possible choice is 2 and then that means that 1 was the number doubled.

Clue number 8 tells us that the hundreds digit is greater than 5.

Which of our possible choices is greater than 5?

The final clue tells us that the sum of all the digits is 15.

Which of our possible digits in the tens place will give us a total of 15?

   2   1   , 8   4   0
   2   (2 x 1 = 2) 8   8   0
                       4   4   5
                       8   8

Hidden Number (Case 1)

1. I am a five digit odd number.
2. Three of my digits are even.
3. My ten-thousands digit is not prime.
4. Two of my digits are composite.
5. The product of 5 and my ones digit is twenty-five.
6. My thousands digit is one less than my ones digit.
7. I am divisible by 5.
8. My ten-thousands digit is not composite.
9. Double my tens digit equals my thousands digit.
10. The product of my tens digit and my thousands digit equals my hundreds digit.

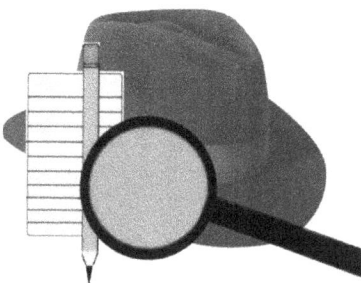

Hidden Number (Case 2)

1. My tens digit is not composite.
2. All of my digits are even.
3. I am a five digit number.
4. All of my digits are less than seven.
5. The sum of my digits is 20.
6. My tens digit is an even prime number.
7. My hundreds digit is equal to my tens digit doubled.
8. All of the digits in my thousands period are the same as my hundreds digit.
9. My ones digit is equal to the sum of my tens and my hundreds digit.
10. The product of my thousands digit and my ten-thousands digit is 16.

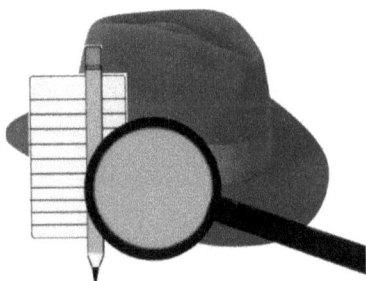

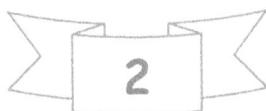

Hidden Number (Case 3)

1. I am a six digit odd number.
2. All of the digits in my ones/units period are primes.
3. The digit in my hundred-thousands place is an odd number that is neither prime nor composite.
4. I am divisible by five.
5. The digit in my ten-thousands place is equal to three times the digit in my tens place.
6. The digit in my tens place is even.
7. The difference between my ones place digit and my thousands place digit is one.
8. The sum of the digits in my thousands period is eleven.
9. The digit in my hundreds place is greater than 5.
10. The product of my ten-thousands digit and my hundred-thousands digit is six.

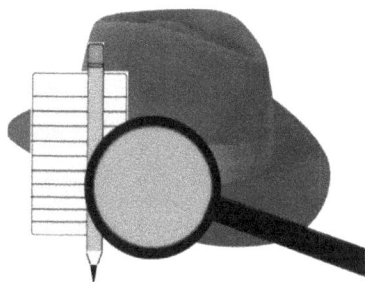

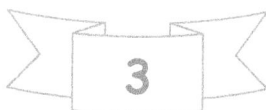

Hidden Number (Case 4)

1. I am a six digit number.
2. The sum of all my digits is 30.
3. My ones digit is a composite number.
4. I am an odd number.
5. My hundreds digit is odd and neither prime nor composite.
6. All of the digits in my thousands period are equal.
7. My tens digit is prime.
8. All of the digits in my thousands period are even.
9. My tens digit is even.
10. The sum of all the digits in my thousands period is 18.

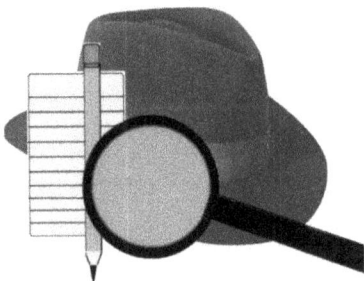

Hidden Number (Case 5)

1. I am a five digit number.
2. My ones digit is divisible by three.
3. The product of my tens digit and my ones digit is 12.
4. I am an even number.
5. My tens digit equals the difference between my ones digit and my hundreds digit.
6. Both of the digits in my thousands period are odd.
7. The sum of all my digits is 22.
8. My ten-thousands digit is divisible by three.
9. The difference between the digits in my thousands period is eight.
10. My thousands digit is neither prime nor composite.

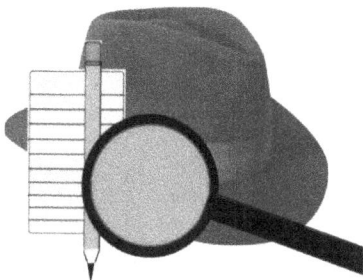

Hidden Number (Case 6)

1. I am a four digit even number.
2. All of my digits are even.
3. The denominator in the fraction $\frac{1}{2}$ is the same as my tens digit.
4. I am divisible by five.
5. None of my digits is greater than seven.
6. The sum of all my digits equals a dozen.
7. My hundreds digit is divisible by three.
8. My tens digit is prime.
9. My thousands digit is double my tens digit.
10. The sum of my tens digit and my thousands digit is six.

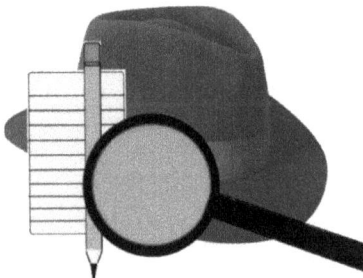

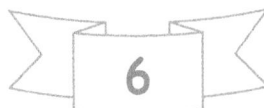

Hidden Number (Case 7)

1. I am a six digit number.
2. All of my digits are prime numbers.
3. The sum of all my digits is 21.
4. All of my digits are less than six.
5. I am an even number.
6. My ten-thousands digit is equal to my ones digit.
7. The product of my tens digit and my thousands digit is 25.
8. The difference between my ones digit and my hundreds digit is zero.
9. My hundred-thousands digit is equal to my tens digit.
10. Three is not one of my digits.

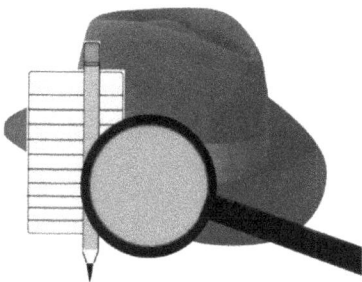

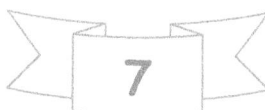

Hidden Number (Case 8)

1. I am a seven digit number divisible by five.
2. None of my digits are prime numbers.
3. All of the digits in my ones/units period are even.
4. My tens digit is double the value of the only even prime number.
5. My millions digit is not composite.
6. The digit in my hundreds place is double the digit in my tens place.
7. The sum of all my digits is 29.
8. The sum of my thousands digit and my ten-thousands digit is 10.
9. My hundred-thousands digit is two less than my hundreds digit.
10. My thousands digit is odd and is neither prime nor composite.

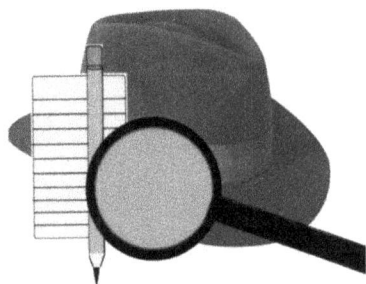

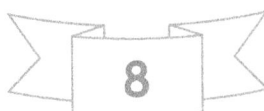

Hidden Number (Case 9)

1. I am a four digit number.
2. All of my digits are prime numbers.
3. The sum of all my digits is 17.
4. I am an odd number.
5. The sum of my hundreds digit and my thousands digit is 10.
6. My tens digit is even.
7. I am divisible by five.
8. The sum of my tens digit and my ones digit is equal to my thousands digit.
9. The sum of my tens digit and my hundreds digit is equal to my ones digit.
10. The difference between my ones digit and my tens digit is three.

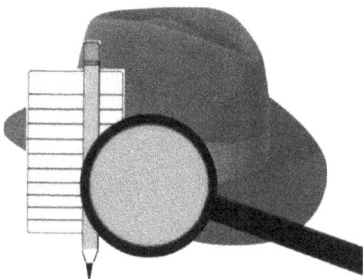

Hidden Number (Case 10)

1. I am an even number.
2. I am less than one-million.
3. My ten-thousands digit is an even prime number.
4. My hundreds digit is an odd number between five and nine.
5. My tens digit is the same as the denominator in the fraction two-thirds.
6. I am divisible by five.
7. My thousands digit is greater than five and has four as a factor.
8. My hundred-thousands digit is not a prime number.
9. The sum of all my digits is 21.
10. The difference between my hundreds digit and my thousands digit equals my hundred-thousands digit.

Hidden Number (Case 11)

1. I am a four digit number divisible by two.
2. My thousands digit is a composite number greater than five.
3. My tens digit is a factor of my thousands digit.
4. I am divisible by five.
5. My thousands digit is odd.
6. My tens digit is a prime number.
7. My hundreds digit is even.
8. The sum of all my digits is 18.
9. The difference between my tens digit and my thousands digit equals my hundreds digit.
10. My tens digit is a factor of my hundreds digit.

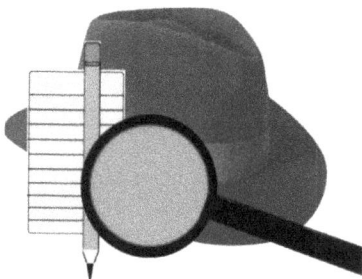

Hidden Number (Case 12)

1. I have a half-dozen digits.
2. My ones digit is a prime number.
3. My tens digit equals my ones digit.
4. My ones digit is a factor of nine.
5. My thousands digit is a prime number between five and nine.
6. My hundreds digit equals the product of my tens digit and my ones digit.
7. My hundred-thousands digit is not a prime number.
8. My ten-thousands digit is less than my hundred-thousands digit.
9. My hundred-thousands digit is not a composite number.
10. The sum of all my digits is twenty-three.

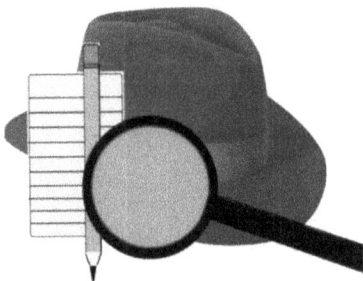

Hidden Number (Case 13)

1. I am a five digit odd number.
2. Only two of my digits are prime.
3. My hundreds digit is odd but it is not prime.
4. My ones digit is a multiple of three.
5. My tens digit and my thousands digit are prime numbers.
6. The product of three and seven is equal to the sum of all my digits.
7. My hundreds digit is not composite.
8. My thousands digit is even.
9. My ten-thousands digit is double my thousands digit.
10. My tens digit is a factor of 25.

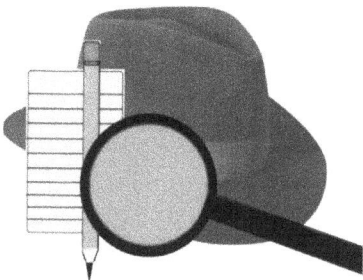

Hidden Number (Case 14)

1. I am an even number.
2. Four of my digits are odd and the fifth one is zero.
3. My tens digit is a prime number.
4. All of my digits, except for my ones digit, are greater than five.
5. I am divisible by five.
6. Two of my digits are composite numbers.
7. My ten-thousands digit is a multiple of three.
8. My tens digit is equal to my thousands digit.
9. My hundreds digit is a factor of 81.
10. The sum of all my digits is 32.

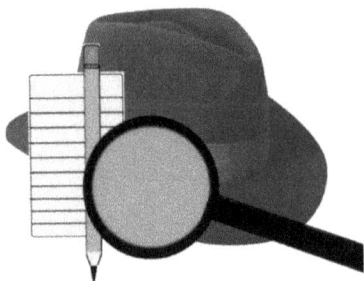

Hidden Number (Case 15)

1. Only one of my six digits is not a composite number.
2. I am an odd number divisible by five.
3. All of the digits in my thousands period are greater than six.
4. My hundreds digit is divisible by two and by three.
5. My thousands digit is divisible by three.
6. My tens digit is even.
7. My ten-thousands digit is divisible by four.
8. My hundred-thousands digit is a factor of sixteen.
9. My tens digit is less than 5.
10. The sum of all my digits is forty.

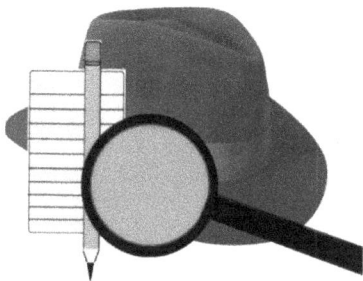

Hidden Number (Case 16)

1. Three of my digits are odd and two of my digits are even.
2. All of my even digits are less than six.
3. Three of my digits are prime numbers.
4. I am an even number.
5. My ten-thousands digit is four.
6. My ones digit is a prime number.
7. My hundreds digit is greater than zero and neither prime nor composite.
8. My tens digit is equal to the difference between my ones and my hundreds digit.
9. My thousands digit is a factor of ten.
10. The sum of all of my digits is thirteen.

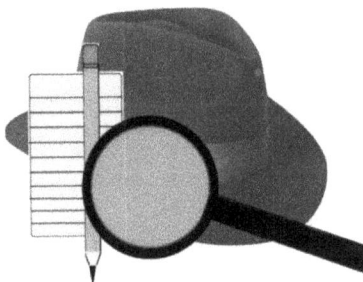

Hidden Number (Case 17)

1. I am an odd number.
2. Only one of my five digits is prime.
3. My ones digit is not composite.
4. My ten-thousands digit is greater than one and a factor of 25.
5. My tens digit is a multiple of two, and of three, and a factor of 36.
6. The sum of the digits in my thousands period is nine.
7. My thousands digit is greater than two and a factor of sixteen.
8. The sum of all of my digits is 25.
9. My hundreds digit is greater than six and a multiple of three.
10. My ones digit is not a prime number.

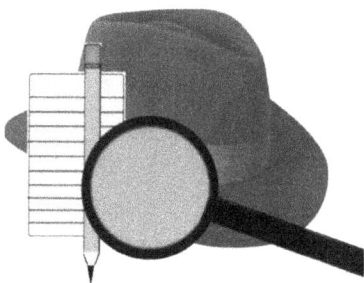

Hidden Number (Case 18)

1. Three of my digits are odd and three of my digits are even.
2. All of the digits in my ones/units period are even.
3. My ones digit is a prime number.
4. My thousands digit is a prime number greater than five.
5. My hundreds digit is double my ones digit.
6. Only two of my digits are prime numbers.
7. My ten-thousands digit is a multiple of three.
8. My tens digit is double my hundreds digit.
9. My hundred-thousands digit is neither prime nor composite.
10. The sum of all of my digits is a prime number.

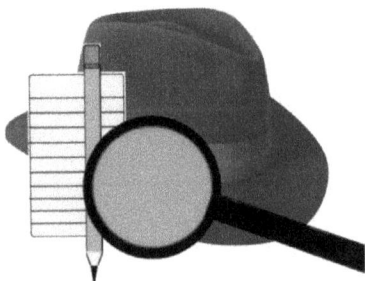

Hidden Number (Case 19)

1. Each of my five digits is greater than or equal to two.
2. My ones digit is between 2 and 6.
3. My tens digit is a prime number between three and seven.
4. I am an even number.
5. My hundreds digit is a factor of 3.
6. My ten-thousands digit is a multiple of three.
7. The sum of my five digits equals the product of three and nine.
8. My ten-thousands digit is greater than six.
9. My thousands digit is a multiple of three.
10. My thousands digit has two as a factor.

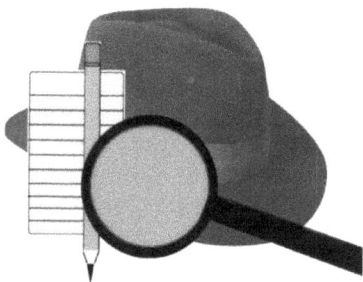

Hidden Number (Case 20)

1. My ones digit is neither prime nor composite.
2. Each of my six digits is less than 8.
3. My tens digit is a prime number and a factor of 25.
4. My hundreds digit is odd.
5. I am divisible by five.
6. My hundred-thousands digit is one less than the sum of my ones and my tens digit.
7. My hundreds digit is a factor of one.
8. My ten-thousands digit is a multiple of six.
9. The sum of all my digits is 18.
10. My thousands digit is an even prime number.

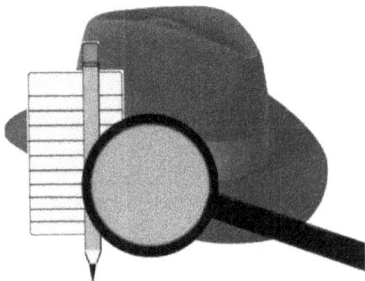

Hidden Number (Case 21)

1. I have a value between six million and eight million.
2. My ones digit is not a prime number but is divisible by three.
3. My tens digit and my hundreds digit are prime numbers and together they have a sum of eight.
4. My millions digit is a prime number.
5. My tens digit is greater than my hundreds digit.
6. I am an odd number.
7. My thousands digit is a composite number with only three, one, and itself as factors.
8. My hundred-thousands digit is even and prime.
9. Double my ten-thousands digit equals my hundred-thousands digit.
10. My thousands digit is greater than five.

Hidden Number (Case 22)

1. I am an odd number with a value between 600,000 and one-million.
2. I am not divisible by five.
3. My hundred-thousands digit is a prime number.
4. My hundreds digit is an odd composite number greater than five.
5. The product of my tens digit and my hundreds digit is less than one.
6. My ones digit is a composite number.
7. My thousands digit is an even composite number.
8. My ten-thousands digit is a prime number and a factor of twenty-five.
9. My thousands digit is divisible by three.
10. The sum of all my digits is thirty-six.

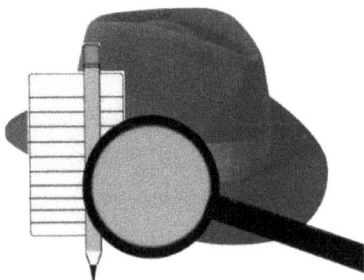

Hidden Number (Case 23)

1. Two of my digits are odd and two of my digits are even.
2. Only one of my digits is prime.
3. I am divisible by two.
4. My thousands digit is a factor of twenty-seven.
5. My tens digit is a composite number greater than six.
6. My ones digit is a prime number.
7. My thousands digit is divisible by three.
8. My tens digit is a multiple of four.
9. The sum of all my digits equals the product of four and seven.
10. The difference between my thousands digit and my hundreds digit is zero.

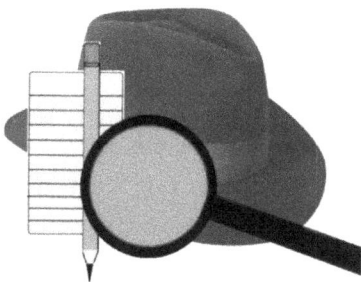

Hidden Number (Case 24)

1. A half-dozen of my digits are less than or equal to three and the other two are greater than three.
2. All of the digits in my millions period are prime.
3. I am divisible by five.
4. I am greater than sixty-million.
5. None of the digits in my ones/units period are odd.
6. One of the digits in my millions period is even.
7. Two of the digits in my ones/units period are prime.
8. I have no prime or even numbers in my thousands period.
9. My ten-thousands digit is a multiple of three.
10. The difference between my thousands digit and my hundred-thousands digit is zero.

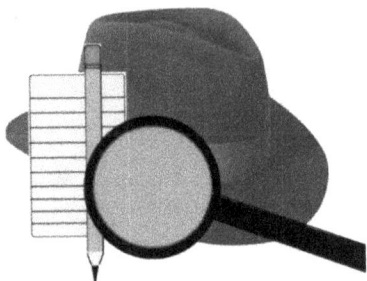

Hidden Number (Case 25)

1. I have a value between 400,000 and 700,000.
2. I am not divisible by two.
3. My hundred-thousands digit is prime.
4. Only one digit in my thousands period is odd.
5. I am divisible by five.
6. My ten-thousands digit is neither prime nor composite.
7. Two digits in my thousands period are prime.
8. All of the digits in my ones/units period are factors of forty-five.
9. My hundreds digit is greater than my ones digit.
10. My tens digit is a prime number and less than my ones digit.

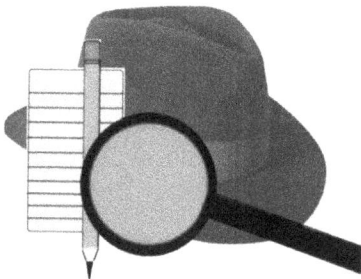

Hidden Number (Case 26)

1. The number of digits I have is equal to a prime number between five and ten.

2. I am not an even number.

3. I am not divisible by five.

4. My millions digit is greater than one and a factor of forty-nine.

5. All of the digits in my ones/units period are composite numbers.

6. My hundreds digit is a factor of my ones digit.

7. The difference between my ones digit and my millions digit equals my thousands digit.

8. The difference between my thousands digit and my millions digit equals my hundred-thousands digit.

9. My tens digit is a number with a value between the value of my thousands digit and my hundred-thousands digit.

10. My ten-thousands digit is an even number that is neither prime nor composite.

Hidden Number (Case 27)

1. I am less than 400,000.
2. I include all the digits between two and nine.
3. I am divisible by five.
4. My hundreds digit is a prime number.
5. My tens digit is even.
6. My ten-thousands digit is a multiple of two.
7. My tens digit is a multiple of three.
8. My thousands digit is greater than my ten-thousands digit.
9. The difference between my thousands digit and my hundred-thousands digit is five.
10. The sum of all the digits in my ones/units period is 3 greater than the sum of all the digits in my thousands period.

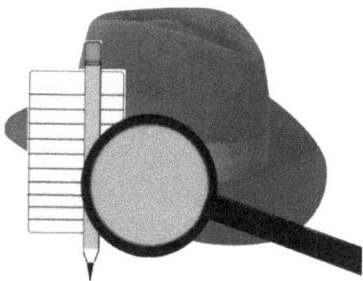

Hidden Number (Case 28)

1. My ones digit is a prime number.
2. My number of digits is equal to the number of days in a week.
3. I am less than five-million.
4. My thousands digit is an odd composite number.
5. Each digit in my ones/units period is greater than five.
6. My millions digit is not prime but it is odd.
7. My tens digit is a composite number between four and eight.
8. My hundreds digit is a composite number and a factor of 81.
9. My hundred-thousands digit is one-third my tens digit.
10. My ten-thousands digit is an even number less than two.

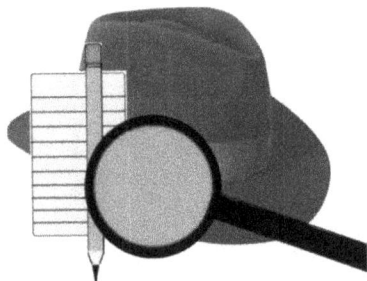

Hidden Number (Case 29)

1. My number of digits is equal to a single digit prime number between the value of a half-dozen and a dozen.
2. I have a value less than six-million.
3. My tens digit is 2 less than my number of digits.
4. I am an even number.
5. My millions digit is a composite number.
6. I am divisible by five.
7. My hundreds digit equals the sum of my tens digit and my millions digit.
8. My hundred-thousands digit is a prime number greater than five.
9. The product of my thousands digit and my tens digit is fifteen.
10. My ten-thousands digit is a prime number with a value between that of the digits in my thousands place and my hundred-thousands place.

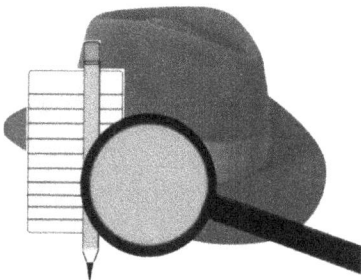

Hidden Number (Case 30)

1. All of my digits are less than six.
2. I have less than a half-dozen digits.
3. I am greater than 45,000.
4. My tens digit is a composite number.
5. I am an even number.
6. None of the digits in my ones/units period are prime.
7. My thousands digit is greater than one.
8. I am divisible by five.
9. My hundreds digit is an odd number.
10. My thousands digit is a factor of nine.

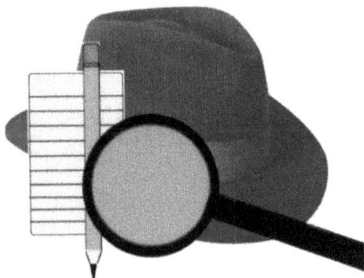

Hidden Number (Case 31)

1. I have a value between 60,500 and 15,500.
2. I am an odd number.
3. My thousands digit is a composite number.
4. All of the digits in my thousands period are odd.
5. My ten-thousands digit is a prime number and a factor of my thousands digit.
6. My hundreds digit has a value between three and nine.
7. All the digits in my ones/units period are composite.
8. My hundreds digit is a multiple of three.
9. My tens digit is less than five.
10. The sum of all my digits is a prime number.

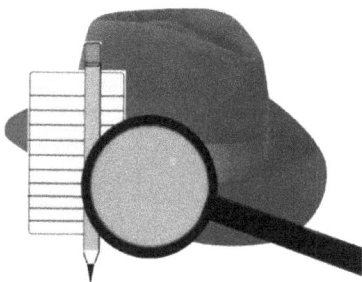

Hidden Number (Case 32)

1. I have, one less than, a half-dozen digits.
2. All of the digits in my ones period are even.
3. My thousands digit is a prime number greater than five.
4. The difference between my ones digit and my hundreds digit is less than one.
5. My ten-thousands digit is odd.
6. My tens digit is prime.
7. The sum of all my digits is equal to the product of three and six.
8. My hundreds digit is double my tens digit.
9. My ten-thousands digit is less than three.
10. I am divisible by three.

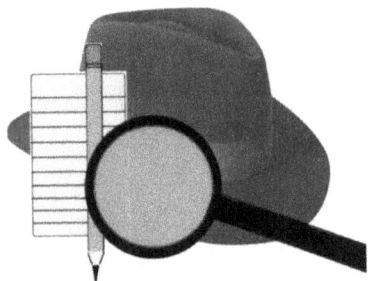

Hidden Number (Case 33)

1. I am an odd number between six-hundred thousand and six-million.
2. My millions digit is an odd prime number.
3. I am not divisible by five and my ones digit is a prime number.
4. My millions digit is a factor of sixty-six.
5. My tens digit is odd.
6. My ones digit is greater than five.
7. The sum of all the digits in my thousands period is zero.
8. My tens digit is a factor of one.
9. The product of my tens digit and my ones digit equals my hundreds digit.
10. I am divisible by three.

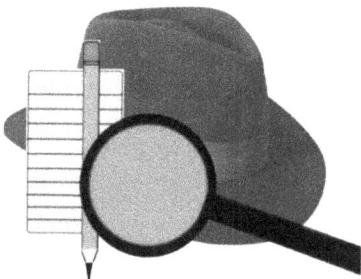

Hidden Number (Case 34)

1. My number of digits is equal to a single digit prime number which is also a factor of twenty-five.
2. My hundreds digit is prime.
3. My ones digit is not prime.
4. My ten-thousands digit is an even prime number.
5. My ones digit is odd and less than nine.
6. Any number divisible by my hundreds digit is even.
7. The product of the digits in my thousands period is zero.
8. My tens digit is double my ten-thousands digit.
9. I am divisible by nine.
10. The sum of all my digits is a factor of 81.

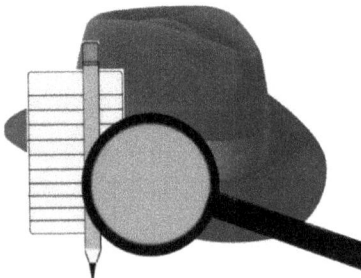

Hidden Number (Case 35)

1. My number of digits equals $\frac{2}{3}$ of a dozen.

2. My millions digit is even and my ten-millions digit is odd.

3. All of the digits in my ones/units period are prime and all of the digits in my thousands period are composite.

4. I am divisible by five.

5. None of the digits in my millions period are prime nor are they composite.

6. My thousands digit is odd.

7. The sum of my tens digit and my hundreds digit is equal to my ones digit.

8. My tens digit is greater than my hundreds digit.

9. Double my tens digit is equal to my ten-thousands digit.

10. My hundred-thousands digit is three greater than my ones digit.

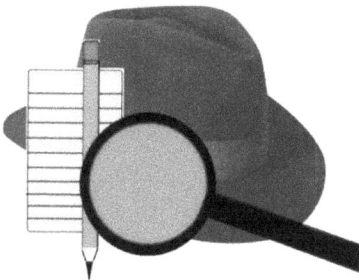

Hidden Number (Case 36)

1. I am less than a million but greater than 500,000.
2. All of the digits in my ones/units period are prime numbers.
3. All of the digits in my thousands period are composite numbers.
4. My hundred-thousands digit is odd.
5. My thousands digit is even.
6. I am an even number.
7. I am divisible by 4.
8. My hundreds digit is greater than my tens digit.
9. My ten-thousands digit is a multiple of two and of three.
10. My thousands digit is greater than my ten-thousands digit.

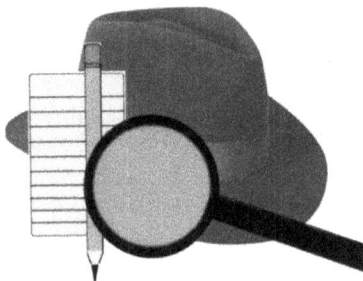

Hidden Number (Case 37)

1. I am a five digit number divisible by eight.
2. Three of my digits are prime and two of my digits are composite.
3. The sum of my ones digit and my tens digit is equal to the first double digit prime number.
4. The sum of my tens digit and my thousands digit is equal to the first double digit composite number.
5. My ten-thousands digit is odd.
6. My hundreds digit is prime.
7. My ten-thousands digit is composite.
8. My tens digit is a prime number and a factor of 25.
9. My hundreds digit is even.
10. My ones digit is a multiple of two and of three.

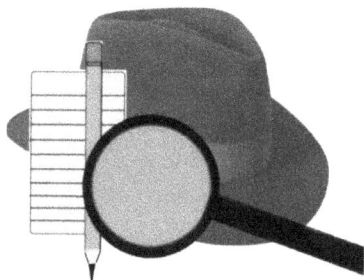

Hidden Number (Case 38)

1. My number of digits is equal to one more than the number of days in a week.
2. All of my digits are composite numbers.
3. Double my tens digit equals my ones digit.
4. My ten-millions digit is odd.
5. All of the digits in my ones period are even.
6. My thousands digit is a factor of 81.
7. My hundreds digit has three as a factor.
8. My millions digit is equal to half my ten-thousands digit.
9. My hundred-thousands digit is a multiple of two and of three.
10. I am divisible by six.

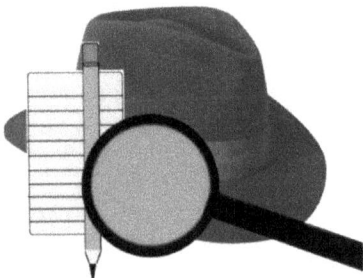

Hidden Number (Case 39)

1. My number of digits is equal to two less than the number of days in a week.
2. My ten-thousands digit is a prime number.
3. My tens digit is a multiple of three.
4. My thousands digit is odd.
5. I have a value greater than 60,000.
6. The sum of my ones digit and my tens digit equals the product of three and five.
7. My hundreds digit is prime.
8. My tens digit is greater than my ones digit.
9. My thousands digit is a composite number
10. I am divisible by four and by eight.

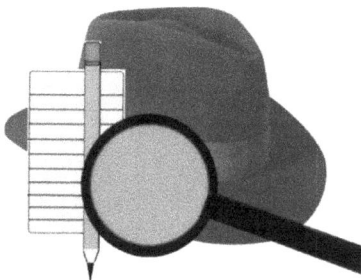

Hidden Number (Case 40)

1. My number of digits is equal to 5 less than the number of months in a year.
2. All of the digits in my ones/units period are prime.
3. My millions digit is composite.
4. All the digits in my thousands period are even.
5. My hundreds digit is a multiple of three.
6. My millions digit is odd.
7. Double my ten-thousands digit is equal to my hundred-thousands digit.
8. Double my thousands digit is equal to my ten-thousands digit.
9. I am divisible by eight.
10. The difference between my ones digit and my tens digit equals my hundreds digit.

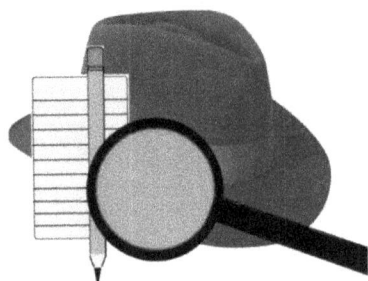

Hidden Number (Case 41)

1. My number of digits is one greater than a half-dozen.

2. All of the digits in my ones period are between one and four.

3. My hundreds digit is odd.

4. My millions digit is odd and less than five.

5. I am divisible by four.

6. All of the digits in my thousands period are multiples of three.

7. My thousands digit is an odd composite number.

8. The sum of my hundred-thousands digit and my ten-thousands digit equals my thousands digit.

9. My hundred-thousands digit is less than my ten-thousands digit.

10. My millions digit is a prime number.

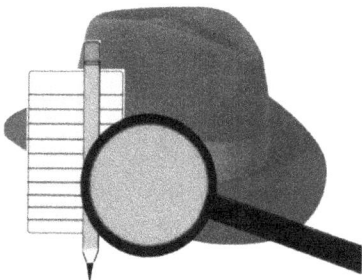

Hidden Number (Case 42)

1. My number of digits is equal to one less than half the number of months in a year.
2. My thousands digit is a prime number greater than five.
3. My ones digit is a prime number less than five.
4. My tens digit is a prime number.
5. The difference between my thousands-digit and my ten-thousands digit is one.
6. The difference between my ones digit and my hundreds digit is one.
7. My tens digit is a factor of twenty-five.
8. My hundreds digit is greater than my ones digit.
9. My ten-thousands digit is a factor of 64.
10. I am divisible by nine.

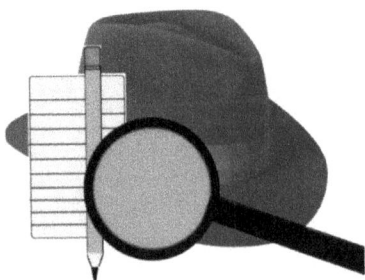

Hidden Number (Case 43)

1.   I am an even number divisible by 5, 6, 8, and 9 and my number of digits is equal to the number of months in a year.

2.   All of the digits in my billions period are odd and greater than one, but only my hundred-billions digit is composite.

3.   My ones digit and my tens digit are equal (the same).

4.   My ten-billions digit is greater than my billions digit and the difference between the two is 4.

5.   My hundreds digit is equal to double the value of an even prime number.

6.   My hundred-millions digit is odd and neither prime nor composite.

7.   My ten-millions digit is an even composite number less than five.

8.   My millions digit is equal to the sum of my hundred-millions digit and my ten-millions digits.

9.   All of the digits in my thousands period are equal, (the same), as my hundreds digit.

10. The sum of all the digits in my thousands period is twelve.

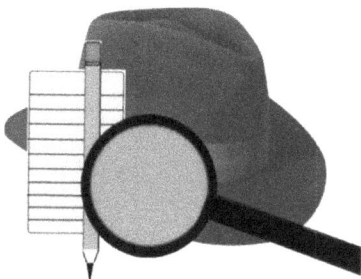

Gumshoe Jargon

Composite Number: *A number with more than two factors (Example: The factors of 6 are 1 x 6 and 2 x 3 so 6 is composite).*

Denominator: *In a fraction, the denominator is the number below the fraction bar that tells how many equal parts are in the whole.*

Digit: *The symbols we use to write numbers and they are 0, 1, 2, 3, 4, 5, 6, 7, 8, 9.*

Dozen: *A set or group of twelve.*

Even Number: *A number that ends in 0, 2, 4, 6, or 8, and can be divided evenly by two.*

Factors: *Factors are numbers you multiply together to get a product.*

Fraction: *A number that names a part of a whole.*

Numerator: *In a fraction, the numerator is the number above the fraction bar that tells what part of the whole is being referred to.*

Odd Number: *A number that ends in 1, 3, 5, 7, or 9, which cannot be divided evenly by two.*

Period: *A group of three place value places (ones, tens, hundreds). Examples are the ones/units period, thousands period, etc.*

Place Value: *The value that a digit has because of where it's placed in a period.*

Prime Number: *A prime number is a number that has only two factors, which are, 1 and the number itself. (Example: 1 x 7 = 7)*

Divisibility Rules

Divisible by 2: Any even number that ends in 0, 2, 4, 6, or 8 is divisible by 2.

Divisible by 3: Add up all the digits in the number and if the sum is divisible by three so is the number (Example: 135, 1 + 3 + 5 = 9 and since 9 is divisible by three so is 135).

Divisible by 4: If the last two digits in the number are divisible by 4, so is the number (Example: 316, since 16 is divisible by 4 so is 316).

Divisible by 5: Any number that ends in 0 or 5 is divisible by 5.

Divisible by 6: Any number that is divisible by 2 and by 3 is also divisible by 6 (see rules for two and three above).

Divisible by 7: Take the last digit in the number and double it. Subtract that product from the rest of the digits. If the difference is divisible by 7 then so is the number (Example: For 224, double the last digit 4 and you get 8. Subtract 8 from 22 and you get 14. Fourteen is divisible by 7 and therefore so is 224).

Divisible by 8: If the last three digits in the number are divisible by 8, so is the number (Example: 1,120, since 120 is divisible by 8 so is 1,120).

Divisible by 9: Add up all the digits in the number and if the sum is divisible by nine so is the number (Example: 585, 5 + 8 + 5 = 18 and since 18 is divisible by nine so is 585).

Properties of 0: Zero is considered even and is neither prime nor composite.

Properties of 1: One is considered odd and is neither prime nor composite.

Answers

Case # 1:	14,825
Case # 2:	44,426
Case # 3:	164,725
Case # 4:	666,129
Case # 5:	91,426
Case # 6:	4,620
Case # 7:	525,252
Case # 8:	1,691,840
Case # 9:	7,325
Case # 10:	128,730
Case # 11:	9,630
Case # 12:	107,933
Case # 13:	42,159
Case # 14:	97,970
Case # 15:	889,645

Answers

Case # 16:	45,112
Case # 17:	54,961
Case # 18:	197,482
Case # 19:	96,354
Case # 20:	462,150
Case # 21:	7,219,359
Case # 22:	756,909
Case # 23:	9,982
Case # 24:	72,191,220
Case # 25:	502,935
Case # 26:	7,502,949
Case # 27:	348,765
Case # 28:	1,209,967
Case # 29:	4,753,950
Case # 30:	53,140

Answers

Case # 31:	39,649
Case # 32:	17,424
Case # 33:	3,000,717
Case # 34:	20,241
Case # 35:	10,869,235
Case # 36:	968,532
Case # 37:	95,256
Case # 38:	94,689,648
Case # 39:	79,296
Case # 40:	9,842,352
Case # 41:	3,369,332
Case # 42:	87,453
Case # 43:	973,145,444,400
Back Cover:	712

9 780692 025352